FINDING FOOD AND WATER

Neil Champion

amicus

Published by Amicus
P.O. Box 1329
Mankato, MN 56002

Printed in the United States of America, at
Corporate Graphics in North Mankato, Minnesota.

Library of Congress Cataloging-in-Publication Data
Champion, Neil.
  Finding food and water / by Neil Champion.
      p. cm. -- (Survive alive)
  Includes index.
  Summary: "Gives essential survival tips for finding food and water in
the wild, including how to know what is safe to eat or drink from land,
plant, and animal sources"--Provided by publisher.
  ISBN 978-1-60753-037-4 (library binding)
  1. Survival skills--Juvenile literature. I. Title.
  GF86C43 2011
  613.6'9--dc22
                        2009030889

Created by Appleseed Editions Ltd.
Designed and illustrated by Guy Callaby
Edited by Stephanie Turnbull
Picture research by Su Alexander

Picture credits:
l = left, r = right, t = top, b = bottom
Contents page Oliver Strewe/Corbis; 4 Momatiuk-Eastcott/Corbis; 5l Paul A Souders/
Corbis, r AGE Fotostock/Photolibrary Group; 6 Stephanie Grewel/Corbis; 7 Marc Dozier/
Hemis/Corbis; 8 Martyn Goddard/Corbis; 9 Peter Johnson/Corbis; 10 Clive Druett;
Papilio/Corbis; 11 Oxford Scientific Films/Photolibrary Group; 12 Phil Schermeister/
Corbis; 13 Michael Freeman/Corbis; 14 Tony Demin/Corbis; 15 Phil Schermeister/Corbis;
16t Eric Preau/Sygma/Corbis, b Catherine Karnow/Corbis; 18 Charles & Josette Lenars/
Corbis; 19 Galen Rowell/Corbis; 20l Eric & David Hosking/Corbis, r Herbert Zettl/Corbis;
22 Oliver Strewe/Corbis; 23 Claire Leimbach/Robert Harding World Imagery/Corbis; 24
Around the World in a Viewfinder/Alamy; 25 Index Stock Imagery/Photolibrary Group;
26 AGE Photostock/Photolibrary Group; 27 Roger de la Harpe; Gallo Images/Corbis; 28l
Stephanie Grewel/Corbis, r AGE Fotostock/Photolibrary Group; 29 Claire Leimbach/
Robert Harding World Imagery/Corbis.
Cover: Elliott Neep/OSF

DAD0038
32010

9 8 7 6 5 4 3 2 1

Contents

Staying Alive

Imagine being stranded in a vast, dusty desert with nothing to eat or drink. The sun is beating down, and you're feeling thirstier and weaker all the time. In another day you could be dead. Your life depends on finding food and water—and finding them fast. This book shows you where to look, what to avoid, and how to stay alive in all kinds of extreme environments.

These hikers are walking across the enormous, scorching Mojave Desert in California. You need excellent survival skills to find food and water in the desert.

Polar explorers can pack a lot of supplies into their large backpacks and sleds.

Beware!

Be very careful when using natural resources. Water may be **polluted** with chemicals or may carry **bacteria** that make you ill. Certain berries, plants, and **fungi** look like edible varieties, but in fact are poisonous. Part of the skill of taking food and water from the wild is knowing what not to take!

Be Prepared

When exploring, always take plenty of food and water. This way you will have enough to eat and drink if your trip takes longer than expected, or if you get lost. However, there is a limit to how much you can carry. This is why it is useful to know how to find food and water in the wild.

Use Natural Sources

There are many natural food and water sources, but they change throughout the year. You may find lots of **edible** flowers and herbs in spring, but there aren't so many in winter. Many animals **migrate** in different seasons. Rivers can dry up in hot summers. Be aware of the season when you are hunting for provisions.

This looks like an ordinary edible mushroom, but in fact it's highly poisonous.

TRUE SURVIVAL STORY

FERDINAND MAGELLAN was the first explorer to lead an expedition across the Pacific Ocean, in 1519. The journey took far longer than he had expected. Soon all his food supplies were eaten or had rotted, and the drinking water had turned slimy.

Magellan and his crew got a painful disease called **scurvy**. Starving and ill, they ended up eating rats, sawdust, and old biscuits full of grubs. They even tried to roast leather, but were too weak to chew the tough material. After 98 days they finally reached land.

Water Basics

Every part of your body needs water to keep it working properly. You lose water all the time through sweating and going to the bathroom. This means that you must constantly top off your body's water supply. If you don't, you will become **dehydrated**. This is why it's vital to have a good water supply in the wild.

Danger Signs

The average human body contains about 105 pints (50 L) of water. You need to drink at least 2.5 pints (1.2 L) of liquid a day, and more in a hot climate. This is what happens when your body loses water:

Losing up to 8.5 pints (4 liters)

You feel thirsty and a little sick.

Losing up to 17 pints (8 liters)

Your mouth is dry; you feel dizzy and have no energy.

Losing up to 32 pints (15 liters)

You are delirious. If you don't get water very soon, you will die.

If you are dehydrated and then find water, don't gulp it down or you may vomit. Take slow, careful sips. Keep drinking small amounts throughout the day, even when you don't feel thirsty.

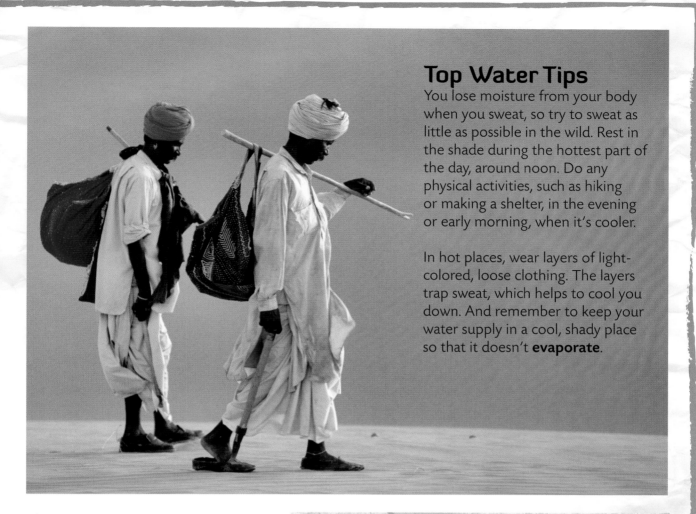

Top Water Tips

You lose moisture from your body when you sweat, so try to sweat as little as possible in the wild. Rest in the shade during the hottest part of the day, around noon. Do any physical activities, such as hiking or making a shelter, in the evening or early morning, when it's cooler.

In hot places, wear layers of light-colored, loose clothing. The layers trap sweat, which helps to cool you down. And remember to keep your water supply in a cool, shady place so that it doesn't **evaporate**.

▲ These men in the Thar Desert, India, wear long, loose clothes that keep them cool and protect them from the sun.

DID YOU KNOW?

You lose water every time you breathe out. In an extreme survival situation, breathe through your nose instead of your mouth—you lose less water that way.

TRUE SURVIVAL STORY

BRIAN K. FOX was a soldier on a training exercise in the Mojave Desert. He and another soldier had to trek across a valley in the blistering heat. On the way, they stopped to check their water supplies and got a nasty shock—they'd left them behind. Fox knew they couldn't go much further. Already he was feeling thirsty and weak, and his limbs were tingling. The men made a shelter, but even in the shade it was unbearably hot. By now, Fox was so dehydrated that he wasn't even sweating. Luckily, a rescue vehicle arrived before he got any worse. He learned a valuable lesson—always carry water!

Finding Water

When looking for water in the wild, try to find a river or stream rather than a still pool of water. This is safer because harmful bacteria can't survive and multiply as well in moving water. Walk up the river as far as you can, since the water nearest the source has less chance of being polluted. Check whether there are animal droppings or dead animals in the river. Both these things will pollute the water.

▼ *Clear, fast-flowing water like this is safer to drink than **stagnant** pond water.*

TRUE SURVIVAL STORY

STEVE CALLAHAN is a sailor whose boat sank near the Canary Islands in 1982. He managed to escape on a life raft with an emergency supply kit and a fishing spear. He knew he couldn't drink seawater because the salt in it would dehydrate him, so he also took a **solar still**. This is a device that removes salt from seawater and makes it safe to drink. Thanks to his quick thinking, he survived for weeks by drinking the pure water from his still and catching fish with his spear. He was rescued after 76 days at sea.

Going Underground

You may not be able to find running water, especially if you're in a desert or other dry place. Don't panic! Instead, look carefully around you. If you can see trees and grass-like vegetation, there may be water just beneath the ground. There may also be water in the ground under dry riverbeds.

1. *If there is a dry riverbed, go to the lowest part you can find. Take a spade or something flat to dig with.*

2. *Dig as deep as you can. Look for signs of the soil or sand becoming damp.*

3. *You can drink water from the ground with a special straw that **filters** water as you suck it up. Alternatively, clean the water yourself (see pages 14–15).*

▲ *This African riverbed is dry, but the green bushes nearby show that there may still be water underground.*

DID YOU KNOW?
*Never eat snow or ice. They will lower your body temperature and could cause **hypothermia**. Always melt them first.*

Animal Clues

Watch the sky for birds, because they often circle above water sources, especially early in the morning or at dusk. You could also try following animal tracks as they may lead to drinking places such as **water holes**. Be careful, because water holes are dangerous places. Other animals may be waiting for a meal. Also, never assume water is clean because animals are drinking it. They may be resistant to bacteria that could make you ill.

Collecting Water

If you can't see any obvious water sources such as rivers, streams, or water holes, you will need to find water some other way. Here are some simple but clever ways you can collect water yourself.

Catching Rain

In rainy places, set up containers to catch rain as it falls. You can also search for rain that has filled holes in rocks or uneven ground. Collect the water as soon as you can, because the longer it has been standing, the more bacteria will be growing in it. In hot places, water will also evaporate very quickly.

Morning Dew

In places with no rain, such as deserts, try collecting **dew** instead. Dew forms during cold nights and is a good source of drinking water. There are several ways of collecting dew.

▲ *In the jungle, large, cupped leaves are perfect for catching rain or collecting dew.*

1. *Leave something metal out overnight. Dew will form on it. In the morning, mop up the dew with a clean cloth and wring it into a container.*

3. *Try this Aboriginal Australian technique. Get up early in the morning and tie cotton clothes such as t-shirts or socks around your ankles. Then walk through long grass where dew has formed. The cloth will soak up water. Wring the water out into a bowl. You can collect a lot of water this way.*

2. *You could also dig a pit and spread plastic on top. Dew will form on the plastic overnight.*

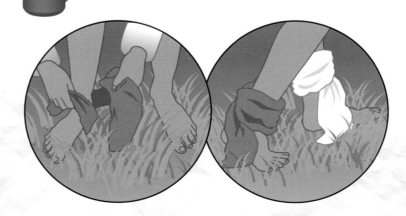

Find a Frog

In the Australian **outback**, you could try drinking from a frog! Water-holding frogs store about a cupful of water under a special skin. They burrow underground, away from the heat, and live off their water supply. Aboriginal Australians had the idea of digging up the frogs, squeezing them lightly and drinking the water that came out from the skin. They then released the frogs unharmed.

These water-holding frogs are burrowing into mud to keep cool.

Water Traps

In hot, leafy places such as jungles, you can also collect water that evaporates from plants.

1. *Tie a clear plastic bag over a leafy branch in a sunny place.*

2. *As water evaporates from the leaves, it **condenses** on the inside of your bag. Only do this on nonpoisonous plants, or the poison may find its way into the water.*

Water from Plants

Many plants in hot places have extra-thick leaves or stems so the moisture inside them doesn't evaporate too quickly. You can cut these plants open and drink the water yourself. Be careful when using a knife to cut tough plants! You must also be sure that the plants aren't poisonous.

How to Cut a Cactus

In deserts, most types of barrel cacti contain lots of water. To get at it, you need a long, sharp knife and thick gloves.

1. *Carefully cut the top off the cactus and scoop out the pulp.*

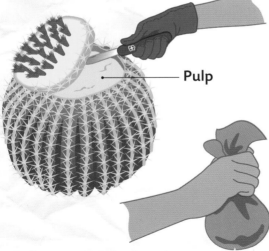

Pulp

2. *Squeeze the pulp through thin fabric, such as cotton, and collect the juice in a cup.*

Another method is to put the pulp in your mouth and suck out the juice. The pulp isn't edible, so spit it out afterwards.

Water Vines

In the jungle, look for thick water vines, which have lots of drinkable liquid inside. Cut off a piece of vine and let the water flow out. You can drink straight from the plant, but don't put the vine into your mouth as it may irritate your skin.

Hidden Water

Many desert plants store water in their roots. Dig them up, crush them, and strain the juice through a cloth. Other trees, such as the Australian desert oak, hold water in the trunk. Aboriginal Australians find ant holes in the tree, then suck the water out with a hollow reed.

Many fruits contain good drinking water. For example, unripe coconuts are full of **nutritious** liquid, which helps keep you healthy and hydrated.

You can drink the water that gathers in the cupped leaves of Malaysian pitcher plants, but beware of insects floating in it!

TRUE SURVIVAL STORY

JACQUES CARTIER was a French explorer. In 1535, his ship became ice-bound near Quebec in Canada. He and his crew spent a terrible winter stranded in the snow. Their supplies ran low and many men died of scurvy. Cartier noticed that local Iroquois people never got scurvy, and he asked them how they stayed healthy. They showed him how to make a drink from pine needles boiled in water. He and his men tried it and in a few days were well again. This is because pine needles contain lots of **vitamin** C, which prevents scurvy.

DID YOU KNOW?
You can drink **sap** from birch trees, or boil it down to make a sweet liquid that tastes a bit like maple syrup.

Cleaning Water

It's a good idea to clean any water you find or collect in the wild. You never know for sure if it contains chemicals or dangerous bacteria, even if it looks clear. There are several ways of cleaning your water before you drink it. Here are some top tips for getting the job done.

▼ *A hiker cleans his water by boiling it over a portable stove.*

The Boiling Method

The simplest way to kill off harmful bugs is to boil water—as long as you have a fire to heat it. Boil it for at least five minutes to make sure you have killed any bacteria, then let it cool before drinking it. If you're high up in the mountains, your water will boil at a lower temperature than normal. This means that you must keep it bubbling for even longer to make sure it's clean.

DID YOU KNOW?
Water that has been boiled for a long time loses its taste. Pour it from cup to cup or blow through it with a straw to freshen it up.

Tablets and Drops

You can buy tablets or drops that kill bacteria in water. Read the instructions carefully. Most tablets need to be dissolved in the water and left for at least 15 minutes before the water is safe to drink. It tastes a bit odd, but at least you know it's clean.

Using a Filter

If your water contains mud, grit, insects, or other debris, you will need to filter it. To do this, you can buy portable filter pumps. They suck water up through a tube and pass it through filters that remove all particles.

▲ *This filter pump draws water up through special filters and into a bottle, ready to drink.*

Make Your Own Filter

If you don't have a special filter pump, you need to know how to filter water yourself. Don't forget to boil it afterwards.

1. *Find some clean cloth, for example a sock, and fill it with clean, fine-grained sand.*

2. *Hang the cloth over a container. Pour in the water.*

3. *The water will drain into the container, leaving any bits trapped in the sand.*

Cleaning Salty Water

If the only liquid you have is seawater, you must get rid of the salt before drinking it.

1. *First, bring the water to a boil.*

2. *Next, place a clean cloth over the container to catch the steam.*

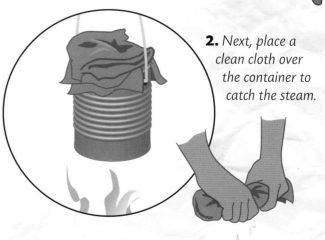

3. *Wring out the cloth into another container. When it cools, this water is pure and ready to drink.*

Food for Survival

You need a good food supply in the wild. It will give you the energy to hike, make tools, build shelters, and do all the other tough physical things that help you survive. Food also keeps you thinking clearly so you can act quickly in an emergency.

This polar explorer is skiing while pulling a heavy sled. It's hard work, so he needs plenty of food for energy.

What To Look For

If you're out in the wild for longer than a week, you won't be able to carry enough supplies. It's then vital that you know how to find wild food sources. The more you can find, the more varied and healthy your diet will be.

There are plenty of plants you can eat, but make sure you know which ones they are. Even edible plants may have poisonous parts. Read pages 20–21 for lots of useful information on poisonous plants.

▶ *In tropical places, fruits such as bananas grow well in the wild and are a great source of energy.*

Staying Healthy

Edible plants contain plenty of useful vitamins and **minerals** that your body needs to work properly. You can also look for ripe, edible nuts which are packed with **protein** and fat. To have a really balanced diet, you should also eat some meat, fish, or eggs, as well as grains. Read more about meat and fish on pages 24–27.

Shoots, Fruits, and Roots

In the spring and early summer, many leaves and shoots are fresh and tasty. Avoid older leaves or ones that have been nibbled by animals. In summer and fall, there is a lot of fruit. Only pick ripe, undamaged fruit. In fall and winter, try digging up roots and **tubers**. When peeled and cooked, these will fill you up and give you plenty of energy.

Learn to spot the leaves of edible tubers. This is a yam, which grows in hot places.

Potatoes grow all over the world and are a very useful food source.

DID YOU KNOW?

Many ordinary weeds, such as nettles and dandelions, are healthy foods. Boil nettles to make a soup and eat dandelions raw or cooked.

TRUE SURVIVAL STORY

RICKY MEGEE was driving across the Australian outback in 2006 on his way to a job interview when his car was stolen. He was left stranded in the wilderness with no food or water. For several days, he kept walking, getting weaker, until he stumbled across a natural **dam**. Megee stayed there for weeks, drinking water from the lake made by the dam and eating raw lizards, snakes, frogs, leeches, and grasshoppers. One day, he heard a truck driving along a remote track, so he staggered into the road to flag it down. Megee had survived an amazing 71 days in one of the world's toughest environments.

All Kinds of Plants

Wherever you are in the world, you can find edible plants. The trick is knowing which ones they are. This is why it's useful to have a local guide who can show you what to look for. And remember, never take all the plants from one area, or they may die out.

DID YOU KNOW?
Even if a plant is edible, it may give you an upset stomach or skin rash. Start by eating just a small amount of an edible plant to see how it affects you.

Desert Plants

Deserts may look barren, but lots of tasty plants grow there. The thick branches, or pads, of a prickly pear cactus are edible, once you've cut off the thorny needles and grilled the pads over a fire. They are chewy and taste a bit like green beans. You can also eat the prickly pears themselves. Other desert foods include dates, wild **gourds**, and seed pods from carob trees, which taste like chocolate.

▼ *Huge clusters of sweet dates grow on a date palm in Tunisia, Africa.*

In the Arctic

You might be surprised at how much food you can find in cold Arctic regions. Shrubs called Arctic willows grow all over the **tundra**. Pick new stems in spring, strip off the bark, and eat the tender shoot inside. Some mosses and **lichens** are edible, such as reindeer moss and rock tripe. They are very bitter, so boil them to improve the taste.

Seaweed Snacks

Lots of plants that grow in the sea are edible. Seaweed looks slimy, but it's full of vitamins, minerals, and protein. Once you've rinsed it and boiled it to a pulp, seaweed can be eaten hot or cold and lasts for days. In Wales, smooth seaweed called laver is cooked to make a traditional food called laverbread. In Japan, chefs use a type of seaweed called kelp in many dishes.

There are three main types of seaweed: green, red, and brown.

▲ *Many Arctic shrubs produce lots of small edible berries, such as blueberries.*

Sea lettuce is a green seaweed with large leaves.

Irish moss is a red seaweed with feathery fronds.

Bladderwrack is a brown seaweed with lots of small, air-filled pods.

Jungle Fruits

If you need food in the jungle, then you're in luck. More than 3,000 different types of fruit grow in rain forest areas. These include bananas, breadfruit, coconuts, mangoes, papayas, and wild figs. Many people who live in jungles also eat manioc bread, which is made from crushed roots of **cassava** plants.

Poisonous or Edible?

Never eat a plant unless you're sure it's safe. It's better to be hungry than poisoned! Even if you think a plant is edible, throw it away if it tastes acidic or bitter. Red often means danger in the natural world, so don't eat unfamiliar red plants or berries. You should also avoid plants with milky sap in their stems, as this can be **toxic**.

Deadly Fungi

There are over 1,000 edible species of fungi. Unfortunately, there are also many poisonous ones. It's often hard to tell which is which, and you can't do a taste test like the one on the next page. The best solution is to only eat fungi picked by someone who is very experienced at identifying them.

▲ *These bittersweet nightshade berries are fine for birds to eat, but make humans ill.*

▶ *Fly agaric mushrooms grow in woods all over the world. Their bright red tops are a clear sign that they are poisonous.*

DID YOU KNOW?
One of the most poisonous plants in the world is called deadly nightshade. Eating just ten berries could kill an adult.

The Taste Test

In an emergency, you may have to take a risk and eat an unknown plant. If so, follow this taste test carefully. **Do not skip any stages.**

1. *Look closely at the plant. Does it look too old to eat? Is it decaying? Even edible plants can be bad for you if they're rotting.*

2. *If it looks fine, take part of the plant—leaves, flower, or stem—and crush it so you can smell it. A smell like bitter almonds or sweet peach can mean the plant is poisonous.*

3. *Rub the crushed plant on your arm. Wait about 15 minutes to see if your skin breaks out in a rash. If it does, the plant probably contains chemicals you shouldn't eat.*

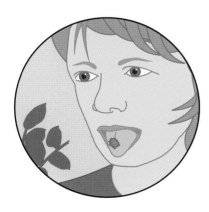

4. *So far so good? Then place a bit of the plant on your lips. Does it sting, burn, or itch? If nothing happens, wait for a few minutes, then put it on your tongue.*

5. *If everything is still OK, then chew a very small piece of the plant. Don't swallow. Spit it out after chewing.*

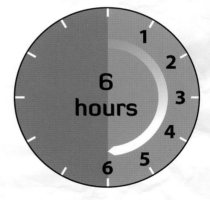

6. *If you feel fine, chew another small piece and swallow it. Now wait six hours. This is how long it takes to prove the plant hasn't made you ill. Don't eat or drink anything during this time.*

IMPORTANT: If you feel ill, drink lots of water and try to make yourself vomit. If you're OK, eat another small amount—but only the absolute minimum. Some plants have low levels of toxins, so the more you eat, the more they build up in your body.

Eating Insects

If your plant diet gets dull, why not try crunching a few insects? They may not look tasty, but many are very nutritious. The only problem is that you will have to collect a lot of insects to make a decent meal. The best solution is to add them to a vegetable stew—then if you don't like the idea of eating insects, you can try to forget they're there!

DID YOU KNOW?
In Thailand, you can buy all kinds of critter snacks, including dried ant eggs, pickled scorpions, and barbecued worms.

▼ Australian honey ants store sweet liquid in their bodies that you can drink.

A Wriggly Meal

Some insects and worms make ideal foods. You could easily survive by eating ants, termites, grasshoppers, beetles, and worms. Just make sure you wash the insects first and remove any wings and **barbed** legs. Some insects can be eaten raw, but it's safest to cook them. Avoid stinging or biting insects and those that are hairy, brightly colored or smelly—they could be poisonous. Ticks, flies, and mosquitoes can carry diseases, so stay away from them.

TRUE SURVIVAL STORY

GUILHEM NAYRAL is a French hiker. In 2007, he and a friend got lost in the Amazon jungle and survived on plants and insects for 51 days before they were rescued. They mostly ate harmless bugs, but then Nayral made a mistake. He caught a large, hairy spider and thought he could make it safe to eat by cooking it. But as soon as he tasted it, the spider's barbed hairs made his lips go numb. His whole mouth swelled up and he got terrible stomach pains. Fortunately, he later made a full recovery.

Great Grubs

Aboriginal people of Australia have a long tradition of eating insects such as witchetty grubs. They dig these fat, white grubs out of the ground and eat them raw or roasted on a campfire. Witchetty grubs are very nutritious and are often given to Aboriginal children because they're easy to chew and digest.

Where to Look

Save time when insect-hunting by looking for insect homes rather than searching randomly on the ground. Carry a container to put them in.

Many insects live under stones.

Lift rotting wood to find insects living underneath.

Look for ant hills like this.

▲ *This Aboriginal woman is using a sharp stick to dig for witchetty grubs.*

Fishing for Food

If you are exploring an area where there is flowing water nearby, then fishing is a great way to find fresh food. You can eat all types of freshwater fish, and they're full of protein. Just make sure that the water you are fishing in isn't polluted.

◄ *The Embera people of Panama fish using long spears. They dive into deep water with the spear or wade into a river, like this man.*

Fishing Tools

You can try fishing with a net, spear, or rod, or even just using your hands. Choose a place where you can see fish, keep still, and be patient—catching fish can take time!

3. *A sock makes a good fishing net. Tie it to a Y-shaped stick and thread wire or bendy twigs around the top to make a wide opening.*

1. *Use cord or string as a simple fishing line. Tie on a hook made from a safety pin or a sharp piece of wood or bone.*

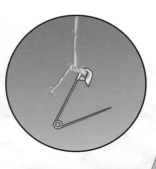

2. *If you have a knife, make a spear by sharpening a stick or bamboo pole, or split the end into several prongs.*

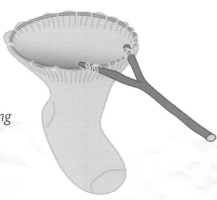

Ice Fishing

Traditional Inuit fishermen in Arctic regions dig a small hole in the ice over water. They then fish with a rod or crouch over the hole with a spear held in one hand, ready to jab any fish that appear. They often dangle bait over the water with their other hand, to help attract fish to the hole.

Gutting a Fish

If you manage to catch a fish, you need to be able to prepare it for cooking.

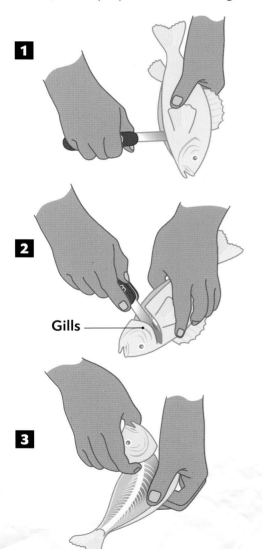

Gills

▲ An Inuit woman fishes with a rod at an ice hole in Nunavut, Canada.

1. *Using a knife or sharp stone, slit the fish up toward the head and away from your hands.*

2. *Separate the head by cutting just below the gills.*

3. *Open the fish and pull the head and bones away in one piece.*

Lots of Seafood

If you're near the ocean, then you can also look for seafood such as mussels and clams. They are all very good for you, but you must eat them right away as they don't stay fresh for long. Shellfish can be steamed, boiled, or baked and eaten out of their shells or put in stews.

Catching Animals

Hunting and trapping animals in the wild can be hard work and often requires special tools and skills. Also, some animals are protected by law against hunters. It's probably best to hunt animals only if no other food sources are available.

Rabbits have excellent hearing and can run fast, so it may be tricky to catch one!

Animal Tracks

Some groups of people around the world still hunt using traditional methods. For example, Aboriginal Australians are skilled at spotting and following animal tracks. Hunters also look for animal droppings, nests, burrows, and paths in the undergrowth that animals use regularly.

Here are a few animal footprints that you might be able to spot in the wild.

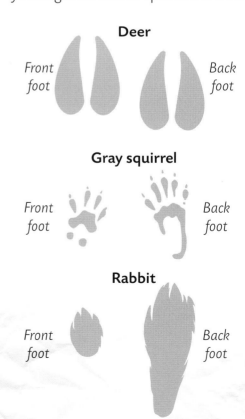

Deer

Front foot   Back foot

Gray squirrel

Front foot   Back foot

Rabbit

Front foot   Back foot

Keeping Quiet

Humans are noisy as they move around, and animals are quick to run away or hide if someone is near. To catch animals, expert hunters slow down, tread softly, and scan the ground carefully for signs of life. The San people of southern Africa are skilled trackers who follow animals over huge distances, moving silently and keeping out of sight.

▶ *These San hunters in South Africa stay close to the ground as they follow animal tracks.*

1. *Hold a throwing stick at waist level, with the end in your palm.*

2. *Crouch down as you throw, and flick your wrist so the stick spins away.*

Hunting Tools

Some hunters in the wild use spears or bows and arrows. Another tool is a throwing stick, which is a smooth, curved piece of wood that can be hurled through the air to hit animals. It takes a lot of practice! Some hunters also make animal traps, but this is illegal in many parts of the world.

TRUE SURVIVAL STORY

DOUGLAS MAWSON was a polar explorer from Australia. In 1912, he led an expedition to Antarctica with two friends and a pack of sled dogs. Disaster struck when one man slipped and fell down a deep crevasse, along with their food supplies. There was no way he could be saved. Without food, the two other men had to kill and eat their dogs. They didn't know that dog livers contain a lot of vitamin A, which makes you ill if you eat too much. Both men became sick. Douglas Mawson survived, but his friend died before they got to safety.

Test Your Survival Skills

Are you ready to find your own food and water in the wild? Take this quiz and discover whether you've learned the skills you'll need to survive. You can find the answers on page 32.

1. What's the simplest way to make sure water is safe to drink?
a) Filtering
b) Boiling
c) Freezing
d) Evaporating

2. If you're not sure whether a mushroom is edible, what should you do?
a) Rub a small amount on your lips.
b) Chop it into tiny pieces and add it to a stew.
c) Leave it alone—don't risk it!
d) See if it's got a red cap—if not, it's fine.

3. You only have one bottle of water left. What should you do?
a) Drink it all at once. It will refresh you more.
b) Save it until you're really thirsty.
c) Drink small amounts throughout the day.
d) Drink half of it, and splash the rest on your face to keep you cool.

4. Where's the best place to collect water here?

a) Source

b) Bottom of waterfall

c) Flowing stream

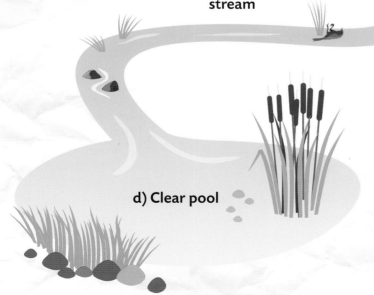

d) Clear pool

5. You're lost and starving, so you do a taste test on an unknown plant. You swallow a small piece. How long should you wait before having more?
a) Six hours, without food or water.
b) Six hours, with lots of water.
c) Three hours, with no food.
d) Overnight.

6. Which of these plants is poisonous?
a) Cassava root
b) Rock tripe
c) Bladderwrack
d) Bittersweet nightshade

7. Don't eat insects that are...
a) Slimy
b) Winged
c) Hairy
d) Fast-moving

8. Which of these things should you NOT do in the desert?
a) Dig for water in a dry river bed.
b) Roast prickly pear cactus pads.
c) Eat the pulp of a barrel cactus.
d) Pick dates from date palms.

9. Which of these plants is safest to eat?

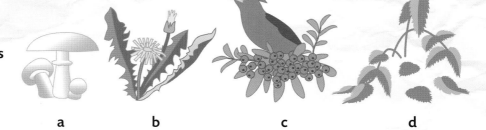

a   b   c   d

10. What kind of tasty insects is this Aboriginal woman digging for?
a) Giant earthworms
b) Witchetty grubs
c) Burrowing crickets
d) Red ants

11. Whose footprints are these?
a) Gray squirrel
b) Rabbit
c) Fox
d) Ferret

12. Don't drink water directly from the sea because it causes...
a) Scurvy
b) Hypothermia
c) Dehydration
d) Seaweed poisoning

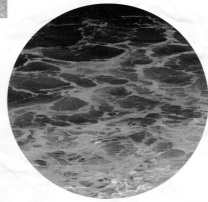

Glossary

bacteria   Tiny, single-celled living things. Some bacteria are harmless, but others cause diseases.

barbed   Having sharp, protective hairs or spines that usually point down or backward.

cassava   A shrubby, tropical plant with thick, edible roots. Another name for cassava is manioc.

condense   To change from a gas or vapor into liquid. Water evaporates from plants as vapor and condenses into water droplets as it cools.

dam   A barrier laid across a river that blocks the flow of water to create a lake. Dams can be built with materials such as concrete or formed naturally from earth and debris.

dehydrated   Suffering from an excessive loss of water from your body. This means that your body can't work properly. Take regular sips of water to avoid becoming dehydrated.

dew   Water vapor that has condensed on cool surfaces, such as metal. This usually happens at night, when the temperature drops.

edible   Suitable to be eaten.

evaporate   To change from a liquid or solid to a gas or vapor. When water is heated, it gradually evaporates into gas, or water vapor.

filter   To remove solid particles from liquid. This is done using something with lots of tiny holes, such as sand or a very fine mesh, which lets liquid trickle through, but traps any solid bits.

fungi   Living things that are like plants but aren't green and don't have leaves, proper stems, or roots. Some fungi grow in soil and others attach themselves to trees or other plants. Mushrooms and toadstools are all types of fungi.

gourd   A large fruit with a tough skin. Gourds belong to the same plant family as pumpkins and squashes.

hypothermia   A condition in which the body's temperature drops dangerously low because of exposure to very cold weather. Symptoms of mild hypothermia include violent shivering, sickness, and tiredness. Severe hypothermia causes muscles and other organs to stop working.

lichen   A living thing that is a bit like a fungus. Lichens grow on places such as tree trunks and bare ground. Some look like yellow, crusty patches, while others are bushy growths.

migrate   To move to a different place to live. Some animals migrate to new habitats at particular times of the year to look for food or nesting places.

mineral   A natural substance that comes from the earth. Your body needs small amounts of certain minerals to work properly. These include iron, calcium, and zinc. You get minerals from eating all kinds of fresh foods.

nutritious   Something that contains lots of nutrients, which are the natural substances your body needs to work properly. Protein, vitamins, and minerals are all nutrients.

Outback   The vast, dry wilderness that covers large parts of Australia.

polluted   Contaminated with poisonous or harmful substances.

protein   A natural substance found in living things. Your body needs protein to stay healthy and strong. You can get protein from foods such as meat, fish, eggs, grains, nuts, and dairy products.

sap   The fluid that circulates inside a plant. Sap is mostly water but can also contain natural substances, such as sugars and minerals.

savanna   Open grassy land, usually with scattered bushes or trees. There are lots of savannas in tropical Africa.

scurvy   A disease caused by a lack of vitamin C.

solar still   A device that extracts pure water from salty seawater. First, seawater is poured into a container with a clear, curved plastic lid. As the sun shines through the plastic, the water and salt evaporate. Water vapor condenses on the inside of the lid and drips down the side, into a separate cup. This water is then salt-free.

stagnant   Water that is still, without any flow or current, and has therefore lost its freshness and become stale.

toxic   Something that is harmful or deadly because it contains a poisonous substance called a toxin. Toxins are produced inside living things.

tuber   A thick, underground stem or root. Tubers swell up to store nutrients that nourish the plant.

tundra   A vast, treeless area in the Arctic, where the ground just under the surface is permanently frozen.

vitamin   A natural substance that your body needs in small amounts to work properly and be healthy. Vitamins are divided into different groups: A, B, C, D, E, and K. They are found in all kinds of fresh foods.

water hole   A muddy pool in the desert or savanna where animals go to drink.

Useful Web Sites

www.wilderness-survival.net
The U.S. Army survival manual offers chapters on finding water and food, plus many other wilderness survival topics.

www.thesurvivalexpert.co.uk/ FoodAndWaterCategory.html
Discover fascinating food and water facts.

www.survivaltopics.com
Click on the food and water links for great articles about finding supplies in the wild.

http://adventure.howstuffworks.com/ how-to-find-water.htm
Read descriptions of several techniques for finding water in the wild.

Index

Answers to survival skills quiz (pages 28–29)

1b, 2c, 3c, 4a, 5a, 6d, 7c, 8c, 9b, 10b, 11a, 12c